Photographic Souvenir
Old Clydach & District
Volume II

Contents

The Village	4
Transport – Trade	14
Religion	27
Education	32
Military and Public Services	37
Sporting	44
Miscellaneous	49
Acknowledgements	56
Previous Publications	56

© Clydach Historical Society

ISBN 0 9518323 1 X

THE VILLAGE

1. Picture Postcard "Come to Clydach".

2. Wesleyan Church. The boundary between Clydach and the Borough of Swansea lies between the church and No. 87 Hebron Road. Note the public water tap on the wall.

3. View of the canal aqueduct over the Lower Clydach River. Beyond is the River Tawe and the Industrial Zone.

4. Celebration Arch at entrance to the square commemorating the Coronation of King George V and Queen Mary in 1910.

5. The Cook's Arms – demolished for road widening in 1968 The landlord and his son Billo are on the left.

6. View of the Square. First photograph taken in Clydach of chicken crossing road!

7. High Street, right hand house is Lloyd's the Saddler, middle house became Maybery's Dairy & Grocery, next became the Butcher's.

8. No. 1 High Street – Lloyds Bank, with the Post Office next door. To the left can be seen the Fives Court (the only others we know of were in the old Swansea Grammar School, Mount Pleasant), it was demolished in 1935 and replaced by the entrance to the swimming baths.

9. On the extreme right is No. 23 High Street – Lipton's Grocery Store. Later a front was added and it became the Williams' Family Shoe Shop. The bay-windowed house next door (No. 25) became Clydach's first telephone exchange in the late twenties. Note no street lighting.

10. General view from Church Tower. Gater's Shop and Dance Hall (No. 37) is prominent on the right. On the left can be seen the skeletal structure erected by Mr. Job Hopkin (the clinic is there now). Railway bridge and embankment visible in middle distance.

11. Lower St. John's Road, note style of clothing and lone street lamp visible on left.

12 Morriston Place, adjacent to St. John's Churchyard. A policeman actually on patrol! Boundary of Fair Field opposite.

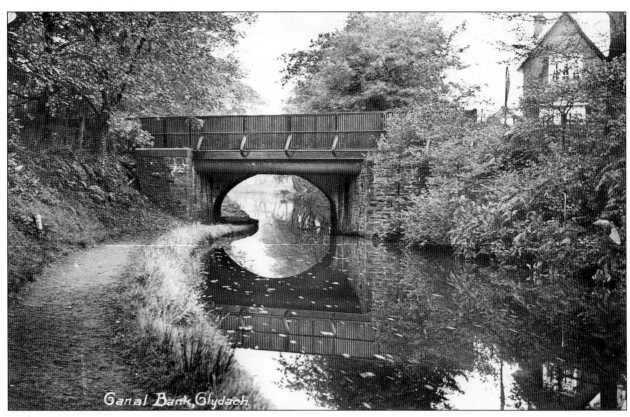

13. The 'Whistling Bridge' over the canal on Pontardawe Road.

14. Ynyspenllwch Road (between Glais and Clydach) enduring one of its many floods. Note fence surrounding Old Mond Sports Field and Entrance Office.

15. The vanished hamlet of Ynyspenllwch. It was here that the first tinplate works in the County of Glamorgan was established circa 1740 – also prone to frequent flooding!

16. General early view of Mond taken from a spot near the rear of the police station. The canal bank, this side, was then a part of Down Farm. The Mond agreed that the cottages in the foreground, although within the boundary of the works should remain in occupation for the lifetime of the inhabitants and subsequently be demolished.

17. General view of Lone Road 1906. The first Mond houses built in Clydach were Nickel Terrace (1902). Built in two blocks of twelve they only had a narrow footpath in between. When it was decided to develop the Sunnybank Estate each end house adjacent to the gap was demolished to create space for Carlton Road. The fields beyond were part of Pen-y-Banc Farm.

18. Close-up of Nickel Terrace in its entirety. The narrow central gap can just be discerned.

19. Panoramic view of Craig-Cefn-Parc with Nixon's Colliery nestling in the valley below.

20. Top end of Lone Road and start of Tan-yr-Allt. In the background is Coniston Hall.

TRANSPORT AND TRADE

21. 'The Stores', 66 Hebron Road, alongside the old 'White Gates' level crossing. In the doorway is the mother of Job & Will Hopkin, great grandmother of Mary Hopkin, the celebrated singer.

22 Jack Ellis, Draper, The Square and his staff. It's interesting how many staff this small but successful business employed.

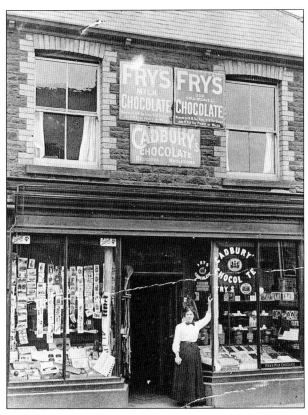

23. Teifi House – home of the oldest extant family business in Clydach. Old Dafydd Jones ran this shop and the gents' barbers next door. The present proprietor Dd. O. Jones (Hair by David) is the 4th generation.

24. Lloyd the Saddler (7 High Street). Mrs. E. J. Lloyd and child in doorway. This business flourished before the advent of the modern motor car.

25. *W. J. Maybery, Butcher (9 High Street). Typical of the era is the plentiful supply of meat hanging outside. The abattoir was at the rear of the shop.*

26. *Job Hopkin outside his decorating business. Later transformed into the Globe Cinema (1912). The large door became the point of entry to the cinema. The shop, for a time, was rented out as a penny bazaar, but later became the entrance to the balcony.*

27. Newbery's, 36 High Street, Fruiterers and Green Grocers. Mr. Arthur Newbery himself in the foreground.

28. Lovering Bros. Shoe Shop, 42 High Street. Today the premises are occupied by Pat Sullivan, Butcher. Note the external lighting.

29. Conti Bros., 51 High Street. Mrs. Ida Morgan's father, Attilio, is to the rear, his two brothers accompany him. When the business moved to No. 53 next door this became Bradford House, W. D. Davies' Drapery.

30. Army & Navy Military Stores, 91 High Street, proprietor Mrs. Hinkley.

31. Shuker's corner shop in Capel Buildings. Note the railway bridge across Vardre Road.

32. E. C. Hopkins' General Store, Craig-Cefn-Parc. This old-established business ceased trading on 12th March 1990.

33. Andrew Delbridge, Cobbler, at Lovering's workshop behind 42 High Street.

Book your Outings with
Eclipse Saloon Services Ltd
AND TRAVEL IN
LUXURY, COMFORT & SAFETY
IN
Coaches Built in Clydach

Catering Arrangements a Speciality

Phone, Write or Call. A Postcard will bring our Expert to your Home with Prices and Helpful Details

Head Office—Capel Road, Clydach

PHONE—CLYDACH 39

34. *Eclipse Bus Co. advertisement circa 1930.*

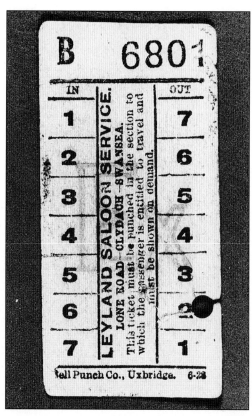

35. *Leyland Saloon Services bus ticket. This service operated from Lone Road in the late 20s and 30s.*

36. *A delightful photo of one of the first S.W.T. buses to operate in Clydach, taken at Nickel Terrace bus-stop. The young girl is Mrs. Kitty Jarvis (née Bailey) circa 1930.*

37. *Clydach Merthyr Colliery Canteen wages slip.*

38. Group of happy Sunnybank residents on Gardiner's coal lorry (suitably spruced up) for a trip to Mumbles.

39. Two Charabancs leaving H. R. Jones' shop for a day's outing.

40. Clydach L.M.S. Railway Station – the Line closed 1953.

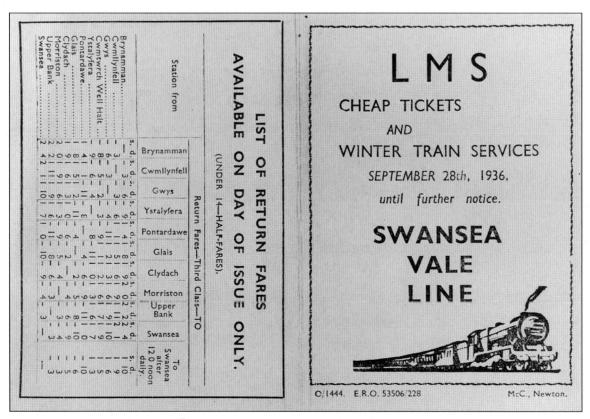

41. 1936 Railway Time & Fare Table. Note that on Saturday afternoons the return fare Clydach to Swansea was 5d. (2p), half fare 2½d. (1p) – very popular with school children.

42. Group of cheerful young workers at Player's Tinplate Works, May 1942.

43. Earlier group of Player's Tinplate employees c. 1900. Note the extremely youthful appearance of three of the boys on the right in the front row.

44. Aerial photo of Mond Nickel Works. The railway embankment to the rear of St. John's Road can be seen. In the foreground is the old Ynyspenllwch Tinplate Works which later became the Canister Works.

45. Mr. Gerald Bellingham, Managing Director, with a group of Player's Tinplate employees on the occasion of unveiling a Percy Player memorial plaque.

46. *A cart load of bricks being delivered for the construction of the Sunnybank Housing Estate.*

47. *Rees' Sawmills, Hebron Road, c. 1914.*

48. Nixon's Colliery, Craig-Cefn-Parc. Group of workers leaving for the last time – 1962. A happy day for the pit ponies anyway!

49. The very last 'spake' of men being hauled out of Nixon's Colliery.

Religion

50. Early interior of St. Mary's Church.

51. Ceremonial procession following the consecration of St. Mary's Church by Dr. John Owen, Lord Bishop of St. David's on 26th October 1905.

ST. JOHN'S CHURCHYARD, CLYDACH, Near Swansea.

2.3.42

For the Burial of Mrs. Thomas

	£ s d
Churchyard Fee for Grave	- 9 - 0
Officiating at Burial Service	- 1 - 0
Clerks Fee	- 1 - 0
Reopening & filling of Grave	1 - 1 - 0
Numbering Grave	- 1 - 0
Paid to James Ford Sexton	£ 1 - 13 - 0

52. Burial bill, St. John's Churchyard, March 1942.

53. A very crowded Clydach Square on the occasion in 1907 of the unveiling of the Horse Trough in memory of Temperance worker W. H. Lewis. It is now sited in Forge Fach Parc.

54. *Rev. T. G. Phillips and Deacons of Pantycrwys Congregational Chapel, Craig-Cefn-Parc, 1940.*

55. *Rev. D. Eiddig Jones and Deacons of Hebron Congregational Chapel, 1906.*

56. *St. Benedict's Roman Catholic Church built 1915.*

57. *Robert J. Jones (East End) with members of his Sunday School Class, Calfaria Baptist Chapel, 1940.*

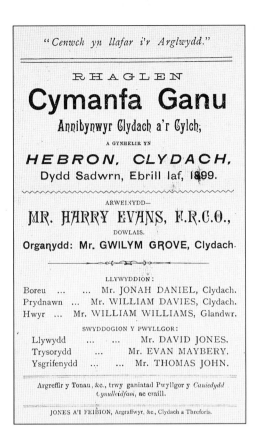

58. Front cover of Hebron Chapel Cymanfa Ganu programme.

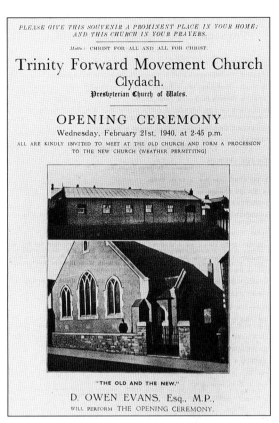

59. Front cover of Souvenir Programme of the opening of the new Trinity Forward Movement Church, 1940.

60. Calfaria Baptist Chapel built 1868. The Chapel is flanked, on the left, by the old Manse and on the right by the new (built 1901).

EDUCATION

61. Clydach Infants' School. It was built by the non-conformists under the 'British & Foreign Schools Society' in 1862. Today it is the third oldest school in the old County of Glamorgan.

62. Also in 1862 the Church of England built the First 'National' school in St. John's Road. It was affectionately known as 'Ysgol Gordon' after the headmaster Mr. George Gordon.

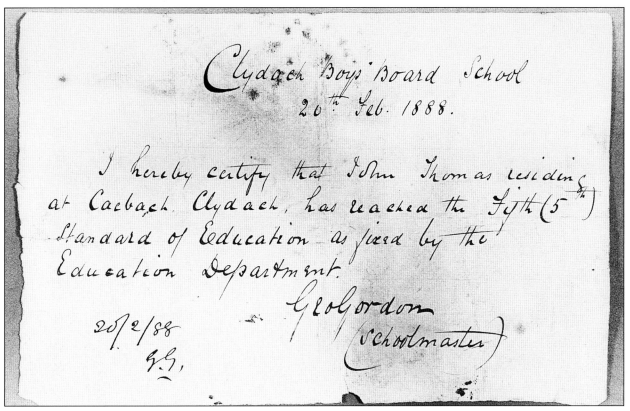
63. Fifth Standard of Education Certificate issued by Mr. George Gordon to John Thomas in 1888.

64. Standard V, B Class (1929), at Clydach Girls' School. Head Teacher Miss Ann Thomas, Teacher Miss Sal Havard Jones.

65. Standard II Class (1927) at Clydach Boys' School. Head Teacher Mr. David James, Teacher Mrs. Baker (née Davies).

66. Standard III Class (1927) at Clydach Boys' School. Head Teacher Mr. David James, Teacher Mr. Rees.

67. Clydach Boys' School Orchestra 1932. Head Teacher Mr. John Butler (right), Teacher Mr. Howells.

68. Clydach Infants' School Teaching Staff 1961. Standing 3rd from left is Miss Tilly Thomas, Head Mistress. The group also contains two subsequent Head Mistresses, namely Miss Mary Jones and Miss Bron Lloyd.

69. Rev. T. Valentine Evans (1861-1935). Minister of Calfaria Chapel from 1882-1927. Wrote 'Clydach a'r Cylch' in 1901, the first known account of the village of Clydach. His eldest son, Emrys, Principal U.C.W. Bangor, was Knighted for services to education.

70. J. Christy Davies (1907-1991) was an accomplished historian who wrote numerous articles on historical facts relating to Clydach and its neighbourhood. His principal local item, entitled 'Clydach' was published in 'The Gower' magazine in 1982 and subsequently re-published by the Society. He published a very comprehensive book on the history of Market Harborough (where he was a local Headmaster) from Roman times onward. He was appointed the Society's first honorary life member.

MILITARY & PUBLIC SERVICES

71. Brigadier Morgan and His Majesty King George VI in North Africa.

72. Brigadier Morgan, H.M. King George VI and General Montgomery in North Africa.

John Gwynne Morgan (1900-86) enrolled in the Artists' Rifles in 1917 and was transferred to the Royal Tank Corps where he was commissioned in 1918. During the Second World War, whilst serving in the R.A.M.C., he was appointed Deputy Director of Medical Services, Middle East with the rank of Brigadier. He commanded the 48th General Hospital at Tripoli and for his services there he was awarded the O.B.E. (Military Division) and was mentioned in dispatches. When Cassino was imminent he pioneered the filter system of dealing with casualties and for this he was awarded the C.B.E. (Military) and again mentioned in dispatches.

During the course of a distinguished civilian career he was in general practice in Clydach and Hon. Surgeon at the hospital for many years. In 1937 he was appointed M.O.H. to the Pontardawe

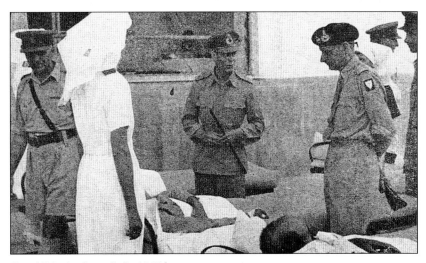

Rural District Council. In 1945 he was appointed Chief Medical Officer to the Mond Nickel Company. He was Deputy Lieutenant for the County of Glamorgan in 1951, appointed a Magistrate in 1952 and Asst. Commissioner St. John's Ambulance Brigade in 1966..

He was a local historian of repute and his hobbies included many art forms.

73. Dr. Gwilym David Watkins (1880-1937) who lived at Vardre House, was a native of Brynmawr, Breconshire. He was educated at Cardiff Medical School and St. Bartholomews Hospital, London.
During the Great War, Dr. Watkins saw service in France in the R.A.M.C. He greatly distinguished himself, being awarded the D.S.O. and M.C. (with Bar), whilst being several times mentioned in dispatches.
Our picture shows Dr. and Mrs. Watkins, with their daughter Joyce, outside City Hall, Cardiff, after he had just been presented his Military Cross.
He was one of the most highly decorated medical doctors in the Great War and continued in General Practice in Clydach until his death in 1937. He is buried in St. John's Churchyard.

74. Pte. Bill Skinner, Sybil Street and Pte. Charlie Spooner, Vera Road of the 2nd Battalion Wilts. Regt., under canvas during the Boer War.

75. Craig-Cefn-Parc detachment of the Home Guard

76. Women employees of Canister Works who served as fire-fighters during the Second World War.

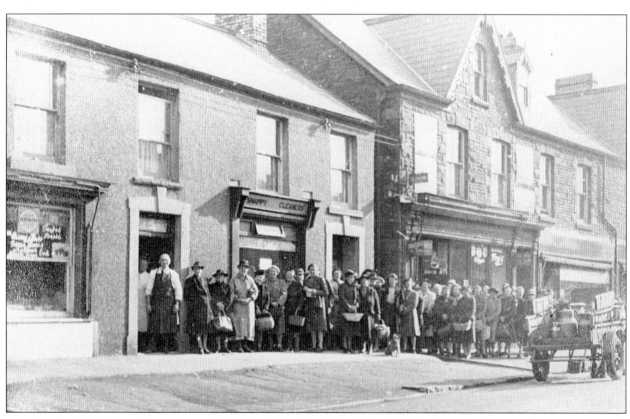

77. A familiar World War Two shopping scene. Queuing for fresh fish outside 34 High Street – Elias Thomas Fishmonger – 3rd June 1943. Rabbits were also occasionally available – free of meat coupons!

THE MOND NICKEL CO., LTD. CLYDACH REFINERY.	297
AIR RAID PRECAUTIONS.	SYMONS, D.R.

Accommodation has been provided for you in

SHELTER NUMBER

29		

Unless you have been detailed for special work, you must proceed to the above Shelter as soon as possible, after hearing the warning signal.

SEE BACK OF THIS CARD

NOTES.

1. The warning signal consists of a series of five-second blasts on the works hooter.
2. Discipline is of primary importance.
3. Take your Respirator with you to the Shelter.
4. Remain in your Shelter until you receive instructions to leave.
5. An identification disc will be given to you in due course. **ALWAYS WEAR IT.**
6. Do not lose this card.

DO NOT PANIC.

78 & 79. *Do not panic! Front and back of Mond Works Air-Raid Shelter allocation card. These were issued to employees during World War II.*

80. *A group of nurses outside Clydach War Memorial Hospital in 1940.*

81. *Hospital Medical Certificate issued in 1924 to B. R. Williams. He was a member of the Ancient Order of Rechabites, Clydach.*

82. *John Player's Works Fire Engine c. 1900. It also operated in the village. It is now on display in the Swansea Maritime Museum.*

83. *Sgt. Scully and his faithful companion. Picture taken in the old Police Station in 1956 on the occasion of his retirement.*

Sporting

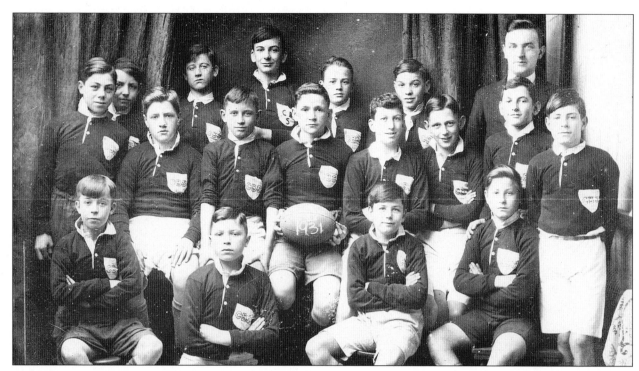

84. Clydach Boys' School Rugby Team 1931. Gwyn Evans (Captain) went on to play for Cardiff and Wales (12 caps 1947-49)

85. Mond A.F.C. 1937. Captained by Arthur Clarke.

86. Mond A.F.C. 1947. Captained by Bob Malone.

87. Clydach Cricket Team, Champions of Division II South Wales & Mon. Association, and winners of the South Wales Evening Post Challenge Cup 1936.

88. A combined Ynystawe and Clydach XI which played a star-studded Pakistan 'Eaglets' touring team at Ynystawe in 1954.

89. Mond Works Hockey Team 1924 with Islwyn Beynon wearing the International Cap he gained that season. He represented Wales on ten occasions 1924-1930.

90. Brian Evans, one of several Clydach cricketers who have won Glamorgan County Caps. A seam bowler, he played for Glamorgan 1958-63.

91. 'The man with the iron jaw!' Dai James fought 450 contests without being stopped. In his very next contest he was stopped by Randolph Turpin after three rounds. Turpin went on to become British and World Middle-weight Champion.

92. Vardre United R.F.C. 1922-23. Captained by Danny 'Post' Williams. The team won the Swansea Senior Championship.

93. Another superb save by Jack Parry. This outstanding goalkeeper played for Swansea Town, Ipswich Town and Wales in the immediate post war period.

94. Beti Wyn Williams (née Preece), Clydach's only Female Hockey International. She won twelve caps in the 1960s.

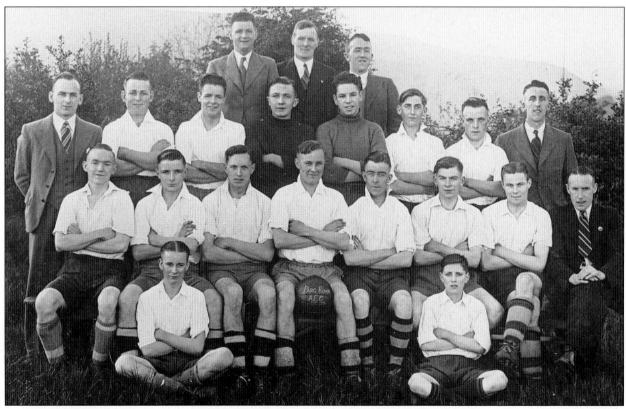

95. Craig-Cefn-Parc A.F.C. 1938. Captained by David J. Bodycombe. Standing, fourth from right, is W. J. Samuel ('Bill Sam') who later switched codes to play for Llanelli R.F.C. As a P.E. Master he became Gareth Edwards' mentor.

MISCELLANEOUS

96. *Ever heard of a shaggy horse story? This one was a star attraction in Bostock's Wild Beast Show at Clydach Fairground in 1926.*

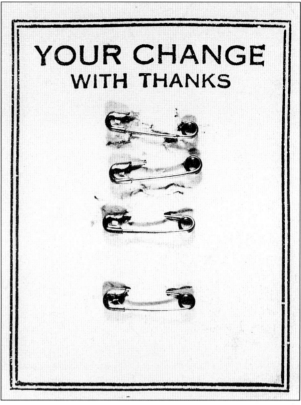

97. *A packet of pins! These were given as change instead of a farthing before the coin was ultimately withdrawn from circulation.*

TOM JONES,
Family Grocer and Provision Merchant,
HONG KONG,
The Square, CLYDACH-ON-TAWE.

Try our delicious Tea.   A real luxury.   You will enjoy it.

DYMA'R LLE I BRYNU TE.

T. Harding, Sons, & Co., Ltd., Bath & Bristol.

98. *Advert for Hong Kong Stores c. 1930.*

99. *'The first cut!' This lovely photograph has been on display for many years in David Jones' Barber Shop, 2-4 Hebron Road.*

100. Clydach Soup Kitchen (held at Salem Vardre) during the 1926 General Strike.

101. A group of retired miners from Nixon's Colliery pose for a photograph outside the swimming baths before departing on their annual outing (1954).

102. A group of happy children celebrating the opening of the new swimming pool, June 1935. Rhyndwyclydach was the first Parish Council in the Country to own its own swimming pool.

103. Washing day blues for Mrs. Margaret Cole in Sybil Street.

104. The Ceremonial Key which was used to open, officially, the British Restaurant in 1941. Miss B. Lambert was the first manageress. The restaurant was sited on the triangle in front of Capel Buildings.

105. *Celebrating the Coronation of Queen Elizabeth II in Sybil Street in 1952.*

106. *This marriage was solemnised at St. John's Church on 25th March 1854. Please note that both bride and groom signed by 'a mark'. This was the rule, rather than the exception, during this era.*

107. The 'Clydach Buccaneers' Jazz Band was highly successful in the 1930s in carnival and festival competitions.

108. Mr. Graham Davies, President of the Society, presenting a commemorative inscribed tankard to Dr. David W. Howell. The presentation marked the successful publication of the 'Nicholas of Glais' book which Dr. Howell wrote on behalf of the Society.

109. Circular 'Beehive' pigsty at Nantymoel Farm, Baran. Following its discovery, Treasurer Richie Walker was interviewed by BBC Radio Cymru for the popular 'Rhaglen Hywel Gwynfryn'. Only about 36 of these corbelled structures survive in Wales.

ACKNOWLEDGEMENTS

The following were kind enough to lend us photographs for publication:

Ted Beckett	Billo Griffiths	Robert Leonard	Ronnie Rees
Joe Byrne	Royston Griffiths	Evelyn Lewis	W. H. Roberts
		Phyllis Lewis	Peggy Robins
Graham Cadwalladr	Norman Harris	Rhodri W. Lewis	Wayne Robinson
Margaret Charles		Georgina Lloyd	
	David James		Sheila Scully
Phil Dalling	Mervyn Jarvis	Dwyfor Morgan	Harvey Sharpe
Mervyn Date	David Jenkins	Huw Morgan	D. O. Symmons
Graham Davies	Elias Gwyn Jenkins	Ida Morgan	
Martin Davies	Winnie Jenkins	Jane Morgan	Aylwin Thomas
Brenda Dewitt	David Morris Jones		Rene Thomas
Tom Dukes	David Price Jones	Ellis Norris	Con Thyer
	Eirlys Jones	Mair Palmer	
May Evans	Gwyn Jones	Peggy Phillips	Richie Walker
	Howie Jones	Sal Preece	John Watkins
Jackie Farrell	Idwal Jones		Adrian Williams
	Jenkin Jones	Archie Rees	Anita Williams
Ron Gardiner	Rhian Jones	Bleddyn Rees	Bryn Williams
Joyce Greib	Rosemary Jones	Freda Rees	Eurwyn Williams

PREVIOUS PUBLICATIONS

1. CLYDACH by J. Christy Davies
2. SOUVENIR BOOKLET
3. PHOTOGRAPHIC SOUVENIR OF OLD CLYDACH & DISTRICT – Volume 1
4. NICHOLAS OF GLAIS by Dr. D. W. Howell

© Clydach Historical Society

President's Introduction

The 22nd April 1993 is the Society's tenth anniversary. I think it opportune that we should now record the facts behind the Society's origins before they are lost. After all we are an Historical Society. The saying "Great oaks from little acorns grow" could well be applied to the Society. After all, five years ago a judicious pruning had to be carried out to control growth. The mighty oak is patently obvious, but first the little acorn had to appear.

A cheerful triumvirate used to meet quite frequently in rather convivial surroundings – and chat! Very often this chat concerned matters historical – local, national or even international. Facts were discussed and debated. Occasionally others added to the discussions and this became an increasingly frequent occurrence. The penny finally dropped and the three realised how much interest there was, generally, in matters historical. So a public meeting was called in the Community Hall on 22nd April 1983. Thus the Society was created and the triumvirate was suitably rewarded – Chairman Brian Ford, Hon. Secretary Graham Cadwalladr, Treasurer Richie Walker. It is a matter of great regret that the late County Councillor Brian Ford will not be with us to witness our anniversary.

As part of our celebrations we publish this second volume of pictures of old Clydach. Our first volume was very well received, so I hope that this will bring you, the reader, just as much pleasure. The vast majority of these pictures were privately owned family snaps, so have never before been publicly circulated. This I believe makes them doubly interesting. To those kindly people, enumerated elsewhere, who have generously lent us their photographs so that they may be copied and returned, we offer our sincerest thanks.

The tremendous photographic task of copying has again been carried out by Neville Turner – without whose efforts we would not have been able to publish this book. Quite a few of his copies are better than the original! It was a happy day for us when Neville joined our ranks. We are very indebted to him. Our thanks to everyone who has contributed in any way to this publication and may you the reader enjoy every moment of your perusal.

GRAHAM H. DAVIES
President
Clydach Historical Society

Secretary's Message

The Clydach Historical Society is ten years old in April 1993. And it only seems like yesterday when more than 120 people turned up for the inaugural meeting at the Community Hall on Friday, April 22, 1983. The Society has gone from strength to strength and is fulfilling the wishes of the founding members in preserving the community's wonderful heritage.

Today the Clydach Society is the largest local historical society in Wales with a roll call of 500 members. Since 1983 the Society has established several milestones in what after all has been a comparatively short space of time. This surely is a reflection on the stature of the Society. Apart from producing a quarterly newsletter of articles on Old Clydach, it has already published a souvenir booklet (1988) containing an absorbing essay on 'The History of Clydach', written by that distinguished historian, the late D. Christy Davies; a 'Photographic Album of Old Clydach and District' (1989); and 'Nicholas of Glais' (1991), written by Dr. David W. Howell, Senior History Lecturer, University College of Swansea.

Now that the Society is in the process of celebrating its tenth anniversary, the committee has decided to mark the occasion by publishing this further volume of photographs of Old Clydach. The celebrations will also include a special illustrated talk by Mrs. Patricia Moore, the eminent Glamorgan Archivist. She has been closely associated with the success story of the Clydach Society from its very beginning in 1983.

It is also opportune here to extend an expression of thanks to Elizabeth Bickford, formerly Archivist-in-Charge, West Glamorgan Record Office, Swansea, Eileen Howarth, the late Merlyn Williams, the late Dr. Gwynne Morgan and Dr. D. W. Howell. Our President, Graham Davies, has elsewhere paid tribute to our founding Chairman, the late Brian Ford.

Over the past decade the Society's Committee has been enthusiastic in fulfilling the aims of collating the community's heritage. We are indebted to those backroom workers.

I would also like to express thanks to all our members and friends for their support in all the ventures we have undertaken since 1983.

GRAHAM CADWALLADR

Secretary

Clydach Historical Society